A Week of Weather

Learning to Collect and Record Data on a Pictograph

D. J. Cortland

Math for the REAL World™

Rosen Classroom™

New York

7 days = 1 week

This chart shows one week of weather.

On Sunday it was rainy.

On Monday and Tuesday it was cloudy.

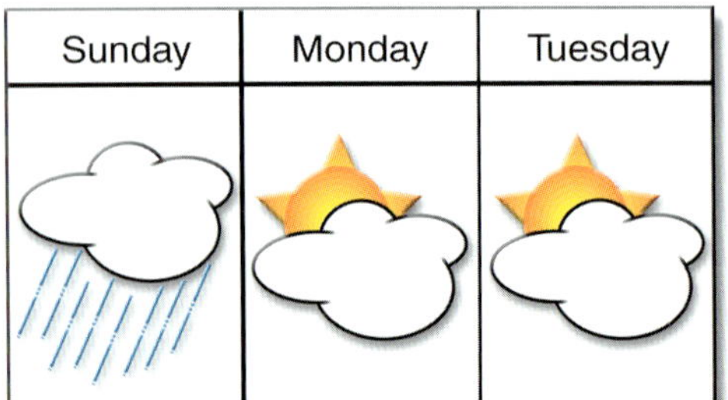

On Wednesday and Thursday it was sunny.

On Friday and Saturday it was windy.

Can you make your own weather chart?

Words to Know

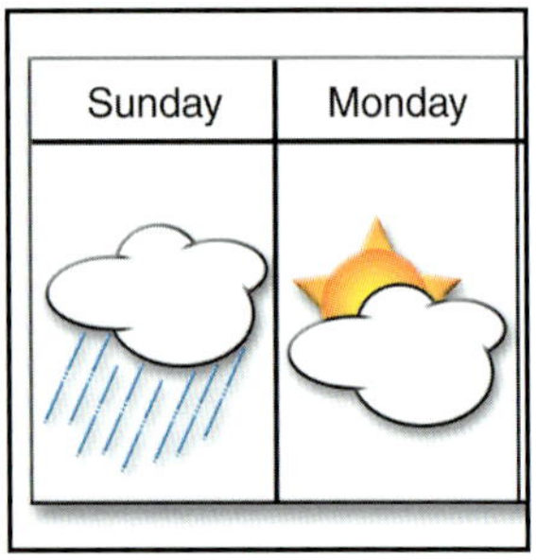

chart

cloudy

rainy

sunny

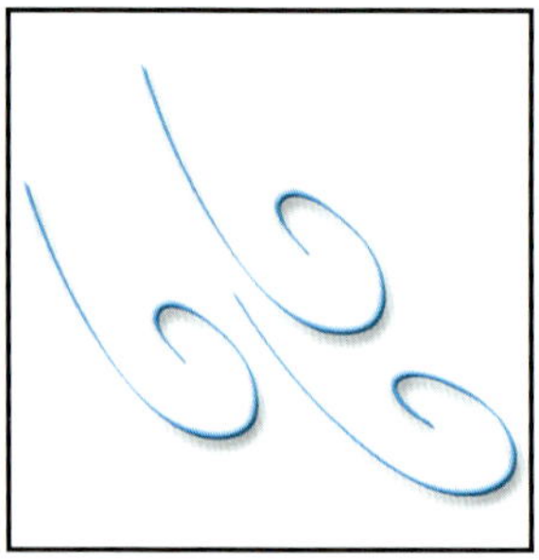

windy